7 Deadly Sins
Of
Your Florida
Personal Injury Case

A Victim's Guide To Florida Personal Injury Claims

Brian S. Brijbag, Esq

This book is not intended to be legal advice nor does it establish
an attorney-client relationship. It is a Consumer Protection
Guide. Please consult with an experienced attorney with specific
questions about your individual situation.

This book is dedicated to all the victims of the negligence of others in the state of Florida. My hope is that something contained within helps you become less of a victim and more of the victor. May this be a pebble to slay Goliath.

Table of Contents

Introduction

Why Write This Book?

The Purpose of my law firm is to "Prevent Injustice by Supporting Victims." This book is a collection of advice I give my clients when they come to me and my hope is that it would be a great help to anyone who is a victim of a personal injury in Florida due to someone else's carelessness. Yet, what this book truly represents is a dive into the directions and the rationale that supports some of the positions I take in my firm – that there is an unlevel playing field in the accident insurance world and a good attorney helps bring things into balance (hopefully even tips the scale the other way!). With that said, the information collected in this book would help any victim, regardless of whether they are represented by an attorney or not.

What Is A Personal Injury?

When you're hurt because someone else has been reckless or negligent, you may have a personal injury claim. A personal injury claim may result from an accident involving either a car or a truck, a motorcycle or a bicycle, or if an individual or business causes injury to someone because there was an unsafe condition in their store or on their property. A wrongful death claim is when someone else's fault or carelessness has caused someone to die. A case of medical malpractice is when someone is injured or dies due to a doctor or hospital's carelessness. So, a personal injury case or lawsuit is exactly as it sounds - an accident that happens because of someone else's carelessness to your person (body), mind, or emotions but not your property (though it may be a related claim). For example, if you are in an outdoor adventure store and a kayak falls off a rack and causes you to break your arm and also break your watch, you could have a personal injury claim against the store owner for your physical harm (the broken arm), but not for the harm to your watch; that would be a separate property claim against the store owner.

As with the watch in the example above, if only your car or truck has been affected in an accident, then you do not have a claim for personal injuries - but you may have a claim for property damage. If both you and your car have been impacted, then you have two lawsuits, one personal injury and one damage to property. Many personal injury attorneys do not manage a lawsuit for property damage unless the individual has sustained injuries as well. That means it may be ideal to resolve the lawsuit on your own if you are in an accident and only your vehicle was damaged and not your body.

For someone whose carelessness causes injury or death, the statute has a different term, it's called being "negligent." Individuals, businesses, and governmental bodies may be held accountable for their acts or negligence. If the incident was someone else's fault, then the injured party could have the right to monetary compensation (money) from the negligent individual. Before any compensation for the injuries is awarded, it must be proven that the reckless person or company that caused the accident was in fact negligent. It must be determined that the reckless person or company owed a duty (to act responsibly towards you), breached that duty (acted against that duty), and their breach of the duty is the reason you are injured. This would make the reckless person or company "liable." Once this is determined, then damages can be calculated.

Lawyers with experience representing injured victims are known as personal injury lawyers. They are trained to:

- Collect facts to support your claim

- Speak with insurance company representatives

- Help you avoid the errors that can destroy your case

- Know when to call in the professionals needed to show the true extent of your injuries.

An experienced personal injury lawyer will help you support your claim of injury at the expense of another's recklessness even when faced with the argument of another side that you are to blame for your own injuries. Your lawyer will also prove who caused the accident by using witnesses, accident analysis experts, and witness interviews to persuade the insurance firm or jury of what really occurred. They know how to build the proper narrative to show the truths of the case.

Florida is a comparative negligence state which means that if it is determined you are partially to blame for causing (or exasperating) your own injuries, your recovery of damages will be decreased by your percentage of fault. While this would not completely prevent you from receiving compensation for your personal injury, an experienced attorney can help you navigate these complex laws.

Florida Statutes Title XLV. Torts

Some of the laws related to Negligence in the Florida Statutes include:

- Section 768.041 (covenant not to sue)

- Section 768.0415 (liability for injury to parent)

- Section 768.042 (damages)

- Section 768.0425 (contractor negligence)

- Section 768.81 (comparative negligence)

- Section 768.31 (multiple at-fault parties)

If you were to pursue your claim yourself, it would be good to be familiar with these statutes. This list is not exhaustive and there are other statutes that may impact your case (like the Statute of Limitations). This is one reason to consider working with a personal injury attorney.

Personal Injury Protection (PIP)

Florida automobile insurance laws require vehicle owners to have a personal injury protection (PIP) coverage of at least $10,000. A key aspect of PIP in Florida is that it provides medical coverage to drivers (and passengers) in an accident regardless of who was responsible for causing the crash. It is important to note that PIP coverage is only available if you seek medical attention within two weeks of the incident for your injuries. Otherwise, you will not be eligible for benefits under the plan. The Florida Statutes list several types of medical providers that count towards the 14-day rule including Medical Doctors, Chiropractors, and even Dentists among others.

Florida No-Fault PIP Insurance Coverage

Florida no-fault PIP insurance covers the following:

- 80 percent of medical bills, including out-of-pocket drug costs, dental expenses and rehabilitation care

- 60 percent of lost earnings

- $5,000 worth of death insurance in addition to the medical and disability benefits offered by the policy

- Mileage compensation for visits to your doctor

Emergency Medical Condition

Under Florida Law, your PIP medical benefits are capped at $2,500 (out of the $10,000) if it is not determined that you have a "Emergency Medical Condition" or "EMC." Florida law describes EMC as an ailment requiring urgent medical attention that may reasonably be expected to pose a significant threat to the safety of the patient. When you've been seriously injured, $2,500 may not entirely cover your needed medical treatment. Florida Law limits the type of medical provider that can make this crucial health determination.

With respect to emergency medical conditions, the Florida law imposes the following restrictions on claims for PIP insurance:

- If you do not get treated within 14 days of the incident, PIP does not pay any medical bills.

- When the initial diagnosis is for a medical condition treated as an EMC, PIP can only offer coverage for follow-up services related to that condition.

- PIP coverage excludes acupuncture and massage therapy but does not exclude myofascial release.

PIP insurance benefits are usually late if they are not paid within 30 days of the insurer being provided with a written notice of the loss insured and the sum of the claim. An insurance provider will have an additional 60 days to examine the claim if the insurer has fair suspicion that a fraudulent act has been committed. Your personal injury attorney must try to ensure that the insurance provider provides the payments owed to you or your medical provider in a timely manner.

Your treating physician can request a Letter of Protection (LOP) from your attorney as you wait for your case to be settled. The LOP normally states that the unpaid medical costs will be paid out of the lawsuit's settlement. This means that the medical provider will not seek to collect any current balance due from you but will instead wait until the conclusion of your case for payment.

You must keep proof of all the out-of-pocket costs following an incident. Insurance companies may be obligated to cover certain out-of-pocket expenses but will not just take your word for it – keep all receipts! For example, to seek reimbursement for out-of-pocket drug costs, the initial receipt for the medication as well as the drug label added to the outside of the medication bag often must be sent to the insurance agency.

PIP Reimbursement For Missed Wages

You must submit a wage and salary verification that your employer completes and then submits to the insurance company to obtain compensation for the missing wages. The paper shows your gross salaries for the 13 weeks before the accident.

Your personal injury attorney can contact your employer directly to ensure that the documentation is filed with the insurance company in a timely manner. The 40% of your wages that PIP may not protect can become part of your claim for damages against the insurance company of the at-fault party. When you are out of work for an extended period of time, the treating doctor may still need to fill in a disability form to seek PIP compensation for missed wages.

Filing A Claim For Damages Not Protected By PIP

Usually, in an accident, you would have suffered significant, permanent injuries so to file a case against the at-fault driver for personal injury. Examples of severe and permanent injuries include:

- Traumatic brain injuries

- Back and spinal cord injuries

- Paralysis

- Disfigurement or permanent scarring

- Amputations

- Broken bones

The insurance company that covers the at-fault driver often will attempt to classify your injuries as temporary and non-serious in nature. They may also look to define your injuries as pre-existing and not related to the negligent conduct of the at-fault party. Your personal injury attorney will obtain relevant medical evidence to prove that your injuries are sufficiently serious to qualify you for damages in a personal injury lawsuit.

Defense Medical Examinations

Auto insurance providers have the right under Florida law to recommend that you undergo an independent medical test (IME) conducted by a doctor of their choice. Despite the name, it is not accurate to define these medical exams as "independent."

Since the insurance company pays this doctor, they may not make an impartial medical opinion when determining the injuries. As a doctor paid by the insurance company, they may be biased because future employment opportunities could be contingent on performance. For this reason, the IME is better termed the Defense Medical Examination.

It is critical, during this medical examination, that you sign no paperwork other than a sign-in sheet without first talking to your lawyer. It is also crucial that during the Defense Medical Examination, you do not talk to the doctor about insurance companies, lawsuits, or any other legal matters. You should note the time the exam began, what was done during the exam, and when the exam concluded. Often you will not be allowed to bring anything into the exam so it is important for you to document what happened as soon as you get back to your car. An experience personal injury attorney can help you understand what to expect during the Defense Medical Examination.

Now that you have a basic understanding of how personal injury laws work in Florida, it is important to know how best to work within those rules. This book will help you by identifying the common mistakes people make and help educate you on the tricks often employed by the insurance company. This consumer guide will often assume that your injuries occurred in a car accident but much of the insight you will read applies to other types of accidents as well. These Seven Deadly Sins can break your personal injury claim and cause you to not be rightfully compensated for the injuries you sustained through no fault of your own. You are a victim and justice demands that you are made whole.

Let's dive right into this guide to helping you, the victim, get the compensation you deserve!

Deadly Sin 1 - Not Gathering Enough Information At The Accident Scene And Not Calling The Police

What details should you get? And what if you aren't receiving all the right information when you're on the scene? The first Deadly Sin is not gathering everything you will need at the accident scene. This important information includes getting the police involved. The crash report will contain a lot of useful information that you will need to make and defend your claim. Let's start by asking what is important to know.

What Should You Get?

Contact Details

First thing you need is the name of the other driver. Don't just go by the name on the insurance card! Maybe the person driving the car isn't the same person on the insurance card? This may be a child, spouse, another member of the family, or a friend who has the owner's permission to drive the car. You will need to know who was really behind the wheel when it is time to state your claim.

Names aren't enough as they may not offer you everything you need to follow-up with in making your claim – try tracking down the popular but generic Joe Smith. You will want to get the address for the other driver too. If you can, copy the details from the driver's license of the other motorist or at least take a photo of the license with your cell phone.

A lot of drivers are more concerned about getting the phone number of the other driver rather than their address and insurance details, but this can be a deadly mistake. You may have to go through the other driver's insurance company to file a claim to get the money you deserve. During this process, you won't be communicating directly to the other driver but instead will most likely be dealing with their insurance company.

If you make the mistake of trying to sort out something with the other driver without contacting the insurance company, there is always a risk that the at-fault driver could just avoid your calls and letters when it's time for them to pay up. Unfortunately, this is how a lot of trusting drivers get burnt. If you have no details other than the other driver's phone number, you may find it difficult to get any compensation for your injuries or repairs to your vehicle.

In Florida, driving without car insurance is illegal. The at-fault driver is required to have a card with the insurance information. It is common today to find that people have an app on their phone with a virtual insurance card. Regardless, you should still get the information yourself. You will want to make a note of:

- The name of the insurance provider

- The insurance company's phone number

- The address of the insurer

- The name of the insurer

- The effective date of the policy

- The policy expiration date

- The insurance policy amount

- Names of covered drivers

- Vehicle details

You should also copy the year, make and model of the other driver's vehicle as well as the registration information. It might also help to write down the license plate number and even the color of the car that struck you. Better yet, take pictures! Often when asked to recall details days after the accident, you will appreciate having this basic information safely collected.

It's also important to have your own vehicle's information, particularly if you're not the car's owner, for future reference. Check your own auto insurance card for the details about the year, make, model and VIN.

Just as important is that you will find the auto

insurance policy number for your own car. You will need this information when reporting the accident to your insurer – or, if you are not a designated insured on the policy that covers the vehicle, if you have to file a lawsuit against the car's owner or driver.

Accident Facts

It is crucial that for you to get the justice you deserve; you must have all the relevant facts about the accident. Some of the questions you should be able to answer include:

What road you were on at the time of the crash?

What town?

What about the crash time?

The nearest intersection?

What damage did you incur in your vehicle?

The other car's driver?

You would be shocked how many victims of accidents do not know this basic information – and how shocked they are to find that they have no answer to any of the first questions that an insurer (or lawyer) would ask.

They are stunned at the moment of the crash and certain specifics can be difficult to note or recall later.

To make it simpler for yourself, take a moment to jot down after the accident:

- The city where the collision occurred

- The road(s) where the crash occurred

- The nearest cross street and any other landmarks

- The time of the collision

- How the crash occurred

- Anything you think might be useful to explain the collision later on

- The damage to all the vehicles involved – not just yours, and if possible, take photos

- If anyone has witnessed the accident, make sure that you write down the names, phone numbers and witness statements.

Much of this would be covered if you take the next recommended step!

Placing The Call To The Police

It may seem like an unnecessary hassle, calling the police after a car accident without seemingly serious injuries. If you are in a large city, you may feel like the police have better things to do or that they will be slow to respond to your call. It may be tempting to forgo calling the police and instead trust that the other driver will work out the issues – car repair and medical concerns – with you directly. Often though, those best intentions do not play out as you may have hoped.

Keep in mind that you often don't know the other driver, and as nice and cooperative as they may appear at the accident scene, it's hard to figure out what their true motives are regarding their responsibilities. Especially if they were at fault for the accident, it's not out of the realm of possibility that they might be playing nice on the scene to persuade you not to let the police write an official report, and later deny any blame.

Rarely do those involved in a collision agree completely on who was at fault. You may think it's obvious that the other driver caused the accident. You hit the brakes, for example, because a child raced across the road chasing after a ball and the person behind you ended up slamming into you. You may not even comprehend how anyone could ever deny they were to blame.

The other driver was at fault in your opinion, because it was their duty to realize you've stopped (and for a good reason) and braked accordingly. But the other driver might say you were irresponsible for unexpectedly locking up your brakes in the middle of the road or even disputing that there was a child in the road. Fault may not be so easy to pin.

Situations like this can get messy quickly, particularly when the teams of both insurance companies get involved. A police investigation and report will cut through the chaos and work against the other driver from moving blame unfairly against you.

A police report can help you establish your medical claim. Not all injuries are immediately reported by the respective drivers. Some take days to manifest, or even weeks. When you find out later that your wreck caused injuries but you did not involve the police, it might be hard to prove with a reasonable degree of certainty that the injury was the result of the collision. The official police report is a key piece of evidence while investigating the other driver's negligence for causing the physical harm that you may need down the line.

Finally, though not as common these days, your own insurance company may require you to have a police report to make a claim. That language may be in your policy and your lack of a police report could bar you from receiving benefits.

For these reasons, erring on the side of calling the police is best, even though it may seem like an undue burden. You may be very glad you did later.

Police Report Details

Once police arrive at the scene of the car crash, they will take yours and the other driver's information down and use it to create a collision report. The report will be essential for you to start pursuing a claim.

Make sure you write down which police department (City, County, State) has responded to your call, the officer's name, and any details on the reports they produced. Some police departments are now issuing cards which contain this information. What's crucial is that, once the paperwork is complete, you know when and how to get a copy. In Florida, there is a portal where you can pay to download the completed report. Keep in mind it may take several days before it is available.

Collecting Incident Details Other Than Auto Accidents

Obviously not every incident involves a motor vehicle. If you've been injured in some sort of incident, such as a slip and fall, dog bite, or if you were hurt on the job, it's always important that you collect all the details you need to make a claim.

Get information about the owner of the property including the name, address, and insurance policy number. Note any persons (such as workers at a company property) who observed the incident. Request a copy of any reports made to document what occurred. Demand that they make an official report! Take pictures of the area to help document the surroundings.

What If You're Missing Something?

Understandably, that is a lot of information to try to remember to get while you may be scared, anxious, hurt, and confused. It can be overwhelming to try to not make a mistake that inadvertently eliminates much needed help.

Luckily, you can also get additional after-the-fact information as the police report that will also provide details about the time and place of the collision, the people involved, and the details about their car and insurance. Gathering as much information as possible right off the bat is often easier-particularly because a police report can take days or even weeks to prepare. You don't want to wait too long to have your car repaired or treated for your injuries.

Remember, call the police for anything but a minor accident and get all the needed information!

Deadly Sin 2 - Delaying Medical Treatment

Auto accidents can change your life and the many responsibilities that come from this change can quickly become overwhelming. The investigation by the insurance company, managing the legal claim, and worrying about the financial impact are only a couple of the things that victims have to face following a collision. Arguably, the most important thing is to get medical attention to restore your health. Delaying medical attention is never a good idea, even though you think you've just suffered minor injuries. There are many reasons why victims of a car accident should seek medical attention. Waiting too long to see a medical provider that understands auto injuries could end up being a Deadly Sin that can hurt your claim!

The Impacts Of Delaying Medical Care

Delaying Care Will Damage Your Insurance Payout

After a car accident, insurance companies are having claim adjusters review claims to ensure that they are legitimate. If you believed you sustained a severe injury, but reports show that after the accident you did not seek medical attention for several days or longer, this may be used by the insurance company as a basis for refusing or minimizing your claim. The insurance company will presume that the injuries were not as bad as you reported, if you didn't seek immediate care.

Gaps in your treatment will give the insurance company grounds to challenge the legitimacy of your medical claim. They can delay payment or offer to settle your claim for less than the cost of your sustained need of treatment. Consistent medical records, which demonstrate a pattern of proper treatment and adherence to medical advice, can be crucial to assure your get the settlement you deserve.

Delaying Medical Treatment May Affect Your Legal Case

In a personal injury case, one of your main claims is that the negligence of the reckless driver has caused significant injuries and other types of damages. As the plaintiff, you must show that the defendant was incompetent and that their negligence resulted directly in your damages. However, if you waited too long after your accident to seek medical attention, the jurors may conclude that this is proof that your injuries were not as serious as you have claimed.

Delaying Care Could Hurt You

The risk of an injury getting worse is high when one does not seek medical care following a car accident. Some injuries take days or longer for visible signs to manifest. An internal injury can reach severe levels before you may have any outward sign of a problem. If after a car accident you postpone treatment, you run the risk of causing a severe medical condition if it remains unaddressed for too long.

Why Would Someone Postpone Medical Treatment?

Why might someone injured in a car accident not seek immediate medical attention? During a car accident, the surges of adrenaline can overtake you and dull the feelings of pain. When you've been involved in a car accident, the body produces endorphins, their own pain reliever. Endorphins can stay in your body for days following your car wreck. Endorphins will make you feel uninjured and postpone certain symptoms of injury. You may not fully realize the severity of your injuries until 24-48 hours, or longer, after the car accident. If you don't feel pain, you don't think anything is wrong.

There are many other reasons people avoid seeking medical attention. Most people just don't know how badly they're injured and think their symptoms will fade over time. Some feel it would cost too much money to go to the doctor and they hope their condition would change on its own. Many people just want to wait to see if the insurance company of the at-fault driver admits responsibility for the crash to provides compensation for damages or medical expenses. A driver may, in some cases, avoid medical treatment if they believe they have a weak case.

Following a car accident, seeking immediate medical care not only protects your personal health and well-being, it also boosts your chances of receiving a fair insurance payout and increases chances of winning in court. If possible, seek non-emergency medical attention within 72 hours. If your car wreck happened on the weekend, however, then you can still seek treatment Monday morning if your injuries are not life-threatening or an emergency. If you feel your injuries are too severe, go to the Emergency Room or an Urgent Care Facility. Following any car accident, it's critical to seek critical medical attention and follow your doctor's advice.

Common Late-Appearing Injuries

Soft tissue injuries are the most common delayed or late-appearing injuries. An injury to the soft tissue may cause a deferred onset of pain. If you suffered from any broken bones, you probably would experience acute pain right away but it is not necessarily the same with damage to the soft tissue. Soft tissue injuries can include:

- Whiplash

- Sprains

- Strains

- Tendonitis

- Contusions (bruises)

- Bursitis

- Delayed onset of pain triggered by endorphins

Soft tissue injuries often have a delayed onset of pain and discomfort due to the endorphins we discussed earlier. Endorphins work with the brain to reduce our sense of pain. Medications such as morphine and codeine work in a similar way. The activation of endorphins varies according to individuals. This means that two people suffering the same degree of pain won't automatically release equal endorphin rates.

No Pain After My Car Crash, Do I Still Need To See A Doctor?

Generally speaking, a professional doctor who understands car accident injuries will always check you out after any car wreck. Regardless of your level of discomfort, or even if you don't feel any pain at all, you should have a physician check you and do a complete examine. Many car accident injuries, such as whiplash and damage to the soft tissue, will take a few days or even weeks to become bothersome. Additionally, soft tissue injuries often cause pain or numbness in areas that are not the origin or source of the injury. Integrated healthcare faculties use a team of medical doctors, chiropractors, and physical therapists to aid with the diagnosis and detection of auto-accident injuries.

Whiplash is another common injury found in victims of car accidents and it can be difficult to diagnosis. It can occur at speeds as low as 5 mph, which can lead to long-term pain especially when care is delayed. If the neck or spine is violently twisted in a back-and-forth motion, whiplash occurs. This aggressive action triggers micro tears in the muscles that cover the neck and chest, which can contribute to swelling and/or rigidity.

Unfortunately, many of injuries such as whiplash and other soft tissue ailments lie untreated for days or even months. Delayed care or care discrepancies may increase the chance of scar tissue, as well as muscle degeneration and arthritis. Get the care you need from a medical provider that understands these types of injuries.

Should I See My Primary Care Doctor After A Car Accident?

It is common for family doctors to have a policy not to treat car accident victims. Although your family doctor knows more about you than any other doctor, when it comes to dealing with the complexity of a car accident related personal injury with possible legal ramifications, your family doctor may not be in the best position to help. Your family doctor will often have a billing policy against accepting automobile insurance, an attorney's LOP, or other options for third party billing. This type of billing for medical services is nuanced and specialized, they may not have the experience to process your claims effectively. Also, your family doctor is often not equipped to document your injuries properly in the medical records to help your legal case or may be unwilling to defend their treatment and the severity of your injuries in court. Finally, your family doctor may not be prepared to deal with the severity of injuries arising from a serious car accident.

Generally, a family doctor deals with commercial health insurance, government insurance plans, or cash payments for services. For injuries related to a car accident, the victim's auto insurance – the PIP benefits – should be billed as primary. Many family doctor's do not want to deal with the additional paperwork (strict timelines, limits on benefits, added documentation, etc.) or they are not familiar with how to properly bill the services. Many family doctors have a horror story of a previous patient they tried to treat through an automobile accident (or they have a peer who has a story), and they are still carrying the unpaid bill on their accounts receivable. Generally speaking, this may not be the ideal place to seek treatment after a car accident.

What If I Did Not Go To The Emergency Room?

There is no requirement that after an automobile accident you need to go to the Emergency Room. Your accident could have been minor, and your injuries don't need an ER visit. Or maybe you've been rear-ended up with significant neck pain, but you don't want to deal with ER just to be sent home with pain medication. A visit to the ER should not have a major bearing on the seriousness of your claim. The emergency department will help assess complications from the car crash but does not offer long-term care. In fact, the ER will usually advise you to follow up following your appointment with a doctor that can manage your on-going care.

Pain Medication And Delayed Treatment

Pain medication, whether over the counter or prescription, can provide temporary pain relief after a car accident. Medication can help to alleviate pain and reduce swelling as a result of whiplash or other severe injuries. While medication in the short term can help control or mask symptoms, they usually have nothing to do with long-term recovery. A lack of pain is misunderstood by many as an absence of deeper injuries, which is one example of how medication can give you a false sense of security and hide the truth. Consistent medical treatment, combined with proper pain control, are the best option for getting better after an accident. Drugs alone can't prevent suffering and distress in the long term.

Theories Leading To Delayed Treatment

"Minimal Damage To Your Vehicle Means No Need For Medical Care."

While we've all heard this misconception before, it couldn't be further from the truth. Most people wrongly assume that the amount of damage to the vehicle is somehow related to the need for medical attention. PIP and No-Fault insurance offers compensation for all of those involved in a car accident, regardless of who was responsible. Yet again, whiplash and other severe injuries can occur at very low speeds, and if left untreated, may lead to permanent pain. Minimal damage can result in severe injury just as severe damage could result in minimal injury.

"If You Don't Feel Pain, Then You're Not Really Hurt."

There's a common belief that if you don't feel pain you were not harmed. Doctors who treat many accident victims, are all too familiar with whiplash and other soft tissue injuries, which can take weeks before the damage is noticeable. Furthermore, Florida PIP requires that you seek medical care regardless of fault within 14 days, and you can use your benefits. Do not be fooled into thinking that no pain means no injury.

"No Broken Bones Means You Don't Need Medical Attention"

Another myth in the world of car accidents is if you did not break something, you are fine. Although X-Rays, MRI or CT scans can detect broken bones and fractures, they are not able to definitely pinpoint soft tissue injuries (with MRIs being the best out of the three for that use). Soft tissue injuries, as already discussed, are the most common type of injury people suffer from auto-related accidents. A skilled medical provider, who has the imaging tools and the experience with diagnosing soft tissue injuries, will be able to document the full extent of all the medical issues that present.

"Lack Of Conclusive Test Results Means That No Serious Injury Exists"

Similar to a delay in the onset of symptoms, visible results on x-rays, MRI, or CT films may not be apparent right away. Over time and degradation, with or without measurable findings, these vulnerabilities can develop into painful problems. Left untreated, whiplash and other injuries to the soft tissue may lead to a life of pain and difficulty.

Many widely known medical issues that result from car accidents include arm and hand numbness, vomiting, weakness or lack of motion, dizziness and memory loss. Some of these medical problems from a car accident could result in permanent, long-term pain and discomfort unless treated in a timely manner. Delayed medical diagnosis and treatment would hinder the rehabilitation.

Furthermore, this delay could be a Deadly Sin that might derail your claim!

Don't Delay And Take These Steps

- Be truthful and don't exaggerate your symptoms. Not every aspect of a medical evaluation will result in a positive finding and some parts of the examinations doctors conduct are intended to decide whether you're faking an injury.

- Be clear about how your injuries impact your health, how they have reduced your ability to work and take part in social engagements, and how your life has changed before and after your accident.

- Document how you feel and be clear about your discomfort with your doctor, what it prevents you from doing and how it affects your job, your personal life, your interests, your daily activities and friendships.

- Create a list of questions during your visit to ask your

doctor and press for answers. When the doctor begins the back and forth, it's easy to forget important questions.

- Keep all medical appointments and arrive on time. Some methods of treatment, such as chiropractic and physical therapy, may require multiple visits a week over a short period of time. Follow the treatment plan prescribed for you.

- Adhere to the doctor's instruction regarding medical care, physical therapy, time off work, and physical limits at work and home.

- If you don't think the medication works, let your doctor know. If you feel as though you're not progressing as you should hope, let your doctor know. Communicate throughout this process. Ask what more therapies or alternatives are available. Some people react to various forms of treatment differently. Medical care isn't 'one size fits all' which is why you need to participate in your plan to recovery.

- Ease gradually back into your physical activity. Doing too much too fast could cause a backlash in your healing process.

- Be patient with the healing process. Your body needs time and restorative care.

- Conclude all medical care prescribed before you are released by your treating doctor.

- Hopefully your injury would be short-term, so work hard at your recovery, but be prepared for a long-term health strategy.

Deadly Sin 3 - Talking To The At-Fault Driver's Insurance Company Immediately After The Accident

Plenty of experts will warn you against talking to the insurance company of the at-fault party. While you need to contact your own auto insurance agent to report the crash, you should take great caution with talking to the insurance company of the other driver. For most serious auto accidents, the ideal way to deal with the other insurance company is to work with an experienced personal injury attorney. Don't commit this Deadly Sin!

Why Should You Be Cautious?

The insurance company of the at-fault driver is not looking out for you. The other insurance company is not your buddy. The insurance companies are financially involved in defending their client's interests as well as being involved in maintaining their own financial interests. To accomplish these two things as best as they can means they work towards refusing outright the maximum number of claims feasible for car accidents and negotiating the lowest possible fee of all other claims that cannot be denied.

Who Is The Insurance Adjustor?

An insurance adjuster is the insurance company employee whose job is to investigate claims and make recommendations on the settlement of those claims. The insurance company is a business which aims to make profits. This is accomplished by lowering its expenses by refusing to pay or by lowering its responsibility for paying. That is the primary objective of the insurance adjuster – to make the insurance company profitable.

This is the goal even though the victim has real and catastrophic injuries. Once they are aware of an accident, they set a value to the claim, even before having the information to understand the full extent of your injuries. They then work to pay the lowest amount possible in comparison. When you have contact with the insurance adjuster, you need to keep that in mind and be highly careful about what you say.

Why The Insurance Adjuster Really Wants To Talk To You

Knowing why the insurance adjuster is so keen to talk to you will help you understand that agreeing to this is often a bad idea. Understanding this will allow you to avoid making an inadvertent error that might damage your claim if you answer your phone only to find out that an insurance adjuster is on the line.

The at-fault party's adjustor will want to get you on the phone immediately after the accident. They want a clear estimate of what the case is possibly worth. This is known as a "reserve value." Good luck getting a payout over that number without a fight. When you speak to the adjustor without an attorney, it is possible that you may inadvertently give inaccurate information that sets an unnecessarily small reserve number. That increases the chances of having to file a lawsuit as opposed to settling your claim. So now you will have to wait months (maybe years) for a resolution and endure the added cost and frustration of a trial.

The first thing you need to learn is that you are not legally required to talk with insurance company of the other at-fault driver. While on the phone, the adjuster may seem friendly and concerned, but he is not your friend. He's trying to get you to say something he can distort and use against you to prove you don't have a fair argument or your case is worth less than you really deserve. Here are some common tactics used to get you to say something or consent to something that could damage your claim:

Pretending To Be Your Friend

The insurance adjuster may sound genuinely concerned about your injury and may make it sound like he needs to quickly process your claim. What he is really doing is trying to make you more trusting of his intentions so you can provide specific details concerning the accident and your injuries that he can use to refute or diminish your argument.

Asking For A Recorded Statement

One of the most common requests is that the insurance adjustor will ask for you to make a recorded statement and will make it seem that it is standard procedure that is innocent in nature. This conversation is captured by the adjustor so it can be played back and used against you at a possible future day in court. The adjuster is a master when it comes to convincing people to say things they did not mean so those words can be twisted around to damage your argument. Do not let the adjuster trick you into giving a reported statement — or a statement of any kind – unless it is expressly required in your own insurance policy.

Requesting A Medical Authorization

Although it is true that in order to settle your claim, the insurance adjustor will need to review medical records, you do not have to sign the medical authorization from the insurance company. The insurance adjuster wants you to sign his form because once receiving all your medical reports, he will go on a fishing trip to look for anything that can be used to hurt your present case. Your personal medical history is privately owned, and the adjuster has no right to access it all.

Friend On Social Media

A modern insurance adjuster's strategy is to attempt to friend request victims of accidents on their social media sites. Do not accept such a request or the request of an unknown person while you settle your claim. The reason the adjustor may do this is to attempt to catch you saying something contrary to your stated claim about the cause of the accident or to see if you say anything implying your injuries are less serious than you report. They may also look for pictures of activities you engage in to twist them to working against you. In general, be highly careful about what you share on your social media platforms before your claim is settled.

Offer A Quick Settlement

When the insurance adjustor acknowledges you have a claim, they may try to get you to agree to an immediate settlement – even before you know the extent of your injuries. If this happens, alarm bells should go off in your head! Often the settlement amount would not cover one MRI let along all the current and future medical treatment that may be necessary to make you whole. They are trying to play into your urgent need for money and your desire not to prolong the inevitable outcome. This conveniently happens prior to your meeting with an experienced attorney so as to take advantage of the lack of understanding the total case position. This initial settlement offer is almost always minuscule compared to the final result steered by an experienced personal injury attorney.

The real reason they want to talk to you is that they want to talk you into committing a Deadly Sin!

Playing By Their Own Rules

The insurance company, whether it was your fault or not, will seek to use whatever you say in the possible lawsuit against you later. Insurance adjusters are well trained to take advantage of what you say about your accident. They are playing by rules that are bent to give them the advantage so remain diligent!

Here's a few sneaky ways they do just that:

- The insurance adjuster will compare the statement you're giving them with the statement you've given the police. They are looking for any contradictions to call your claim into question. It is not uncommon for a person to tell the story of the accident slightly differently once it is repeated four or five times over several months.

- Adjusters will also ask you tough questions that might be designed to frame your answer in a way to hurt your claim. Occasionally, an aggressive adjuster may force you to consent to the accuracy of facts you don't know. You will get angry and say, 'I think so,' to get the guy to leave you alone. Now they have pushed you to damage your case.

- If your car accident case goes to court, the insurance company attorney can use your recorded statement when cross-examining you. You may have given that statement months ago and you may have difficulty recalling what you said. Any inconsistency with your previous statement can be very negative. The defense attorney will seek to capitalize on any uncertainty or contradiction to poke holes in your case.

Not every insurance adjustor is out to get you but know that the risk to your claim is high so it is best to avoid having contact beyond what it required.

When Should You Talk To The Insurance Adjustor?

While not the norm, there are instances where it makes sense to talk to the at-fault party's insurance company without an attorney. For example, if you were in a minor car accident (both property damage and injuries) and the other driver is clearly 100 percent at fault, it may make sense to resolve the matter quickly. If the police report suggests the other driver caused the crash, and it was minor, then you may be able to have a swift and easy resolution.

But if the accident includes any of the following, get a personal injury attorney involved:

- Broken bones

- Hospital/Urgent Care visit

- Long-term health complications

- Medical bills over $2000

- Losing more than one or two days of work / school or daily life

- Some disagreement about who was at fault

- People beside yourself were injured

- Insurance company is playing rough

Your insurance policy may contain language which, if requested by the adjuster, requires you to give a written statement. If that is the case, find out the exact language needed by the contract. Your own insurance company may be the one taking a stand against you! Therefore, you should think very carefully about every fact you give your insurance provider in a reported statement.

Best course of action is to consult with an experienced personal injury attorney before speaking to the insurance company. That way you know your rights are being protected and you can avoid a Deadly Sin!

Deadly Sin 4 - Believing Insurance Company Marketing

What Insurance Companies Do — And Don't Do — When You Are In A Car Accident

What Insurance Companies Don't Do

Insurance Companies don't exist to be your "good friend," to keep you in their "safe hands" or to be "on your side." Dealing with them won't make you "as happy as an antelope with night vision goggles."

To make sure it in plainly understood, in today's

world, whether you've been involved in an accident caused by somebody else or not, the insurance company isn't interested in making sure you are fairly compensated and justly taken care of you by restoring you whole. Your interests and their interests are in fact the exact opposite of each other.

This is the simple version of how insurance companies make money - they bring in the highest amount of premiums they can, hold onto that money for as long as they can, and pay out as little as they can in claims. This is how the insurance business plan works. All those clever and warm-hearted TV advertisements are just that — TV ads.

Beyond that income generating scheme - making money by collecting as much as possible and paying out as little as possible – insurance companies also make large amounts by investing the premium money they collect before they have to pay it out. The money is called the "float." In fact, it is often the case the carriers take in less in premiums than they pay out in claims and still make big net profits. That investment income adds up to real money. Billions of dollars of profit.

Insurance in the United States has come a long way from its beginnings in the 18th Century. Back then, people in a given area pooled resources together and acted in a manner to support those that had experienced a loss. The mindset was focused on building a community support system, not to drive corporate profits. The belief was that if one suffered, everyone suffered so it was best to build an infrastructure to share losses among businesses and individuals. With this being the prevalent thought, the insurance company was aware, and it was expected, that claims needed to be timely paid.

That is not quite how insurance companies operate nowadays. Today's insurance firms are big, impersonal corporations guided by a desire to extract extra dollars out of the compensation process, boost ever-increasing corporate valuation and stock prices, and finance extraordinary wages for millionaire executives.

If you have a soft tissue injury from an accident that wasn't your fault, you are right in the middle of the crosshairs of the insurance company. Contrary to still being that "good neighbor," they will do what they can to maximize their profit and believing their pitch is a Deadly Sin that can torpedo your case.

Claims Handling Changes Over The Last 25 Years

Over the past 25 years, insurance companies have radically changed their way of handling claims, particularly claims for soft tissue injury. State Farm and Allstate, the two largest auto insurers, have led the way. After that, the other corporations followed suit.

Insurance is not like any other corporate endeavors. Insurance carriers are regulated by the States in similar ways to public utilities. The holding of premium money insurance companies which is not technically theirs (i.e., the "float" discussed earlier), is bound in many instances by a duty of good faith. Yet over the last 25 years, insurance companies have purposely placed in place differing claims management protocols designed to push the boundaries of their regulations.

In the early 90's, Allstate hired the consulting firm that helped Enron to overhaul the business model of the claims department. Rather than a focus of providing support and assistance to loss-stricken consumers and claimants, claims became a profit-driven portion of the company based on bogus computer systems that spat out deliberately low offers to compensate victims. These software programs were designed around checking off boxes to spit out a settlement value. Soft tissue claims became a prime target for these impersonal evaluators.

They did not look at reducing the large dollar claims, the ones that resulted in million-dollar payouts, instead the focus was set on soft tissue injuries. Why look here to save money? Because the sheer volume of these smaller claims could easily be whittled down and money shaved off each one resulting in tremendous savings in the aggregate.

The new strategy worked – saving some money on a large number of claims was a better use of business resources than saving a large amount of money on a few claims. The effect was record breaking profit for the insurance companies and ceiling-shattering compensation for their CEOs. The money at the bottom line doubled and stocks rose.

Yet thousands of victims, many the very customers of the insurance industry, were massively undercompensated for the losses. The results of playing hardball when it came to soft tissue claims is trillions to the insurance company and very little to the communities they serve.

While soft tissue claims are being dragged through the claims process, and policyholders are suffering, what is not happening is a reduction in premiums for other insurance customers. The effect of the claim's management reforms of the mid-1990s is the movement from good faith to bad.

Tell Us How Amazing You Are

The irony in this is that just as Allstate, State Farm and other carriers started their unjust treatment of victims of accidents, they embarked on various media campaigns telling us how good they were. Airwaves became flooded with very well-crafted messaging from empathetic to comical – all trying to make us believe that the insurance company was on our side. Well-respected actors used their influence to hawk us savings and service. Talking animals convinced us how easy it would be to switch. All of it encouraging us to put our concerns in their hands.

The main takeaway of all those ads is that the insurance companies are all really good at taking your premium money, and if you miss a payment, their cancelation of your policy will be handled just as efficiently.

After A Disaster, Won't Your Own Company Support You?

After a car accident that was not your fault, you would think that your own insurance company will be on your side and fighting for your rights. Unfortunately, this is a myth that many people will not realize until it is too late. In your insurance policy, there is no clause or statement where the insurance company must defend your position when you are the victim of someone else's negligence.

The insurance company is not going to go to bat for you when you are in a crash. They're built to fight for their own rights and for themselves. For example, when taking on the at-fault driver's insurance company means that your insurance company will not have to pay money, then they will fight. But make no mistake, your benefit is incidental and a happy accident. They are not battling for you; they fight for themselves and for their profit.

The insurance company really has little to gain from quarreling with the other carrier. You are, for all intense and purposes, on your own. Your company, for example, has no interest in fighting to ensure that the other driver's carrier pays you fairly for your vehicle. And they certainly have no interest in fighting to make sure you are paid fairly for your injuries by the other driver's carrier. In fact, many insurance companies don't even explain to their customers how their own policy can help them after a wreck. Or, the carrier will try to dissuade its customers from using valuable coverage that the customer has paid by telling the customer that their "rates will go up." This type of "advice" is possibly illegal, in violation of many state insurance codes, and often costs wounded people thousands of dollars that they can ill afford to lose at a critical time in their lives.

Often what happens is that people contact their own insurance agent and quickly realize that they do not know much about the actual claims process. This is because insurance agents are specialist in insurance sales. Insurance adjusters are the people who specialize in managing claims. This sets up the good cop, bad guy dynamic. The good cop is the local person you know from your church or gardening club who comes to your home and sells you the insurance policy. The bad cop is the adjuster who just comes along when there is a question (i.e., a claim) and then tells you your vehicle isn't worth as much as you thought or your accident isn't really that bad. The carrier would rather have you get angry at the adjuster than at the agent. You do not blame the agent and keep buying insurance from him, even though his colleague just took advantage of you and limited you getting the compensation you deserve.

It is not their mission to look out for your interests after an accident. After an accident is reported, they get to work quickly but not to help you.

The first thing they do is investigate the wreck. This

normally includes getting recorded statements and reviewing the police report. When the adjuster calls you, he or she is not asking to take your statement just for kicks; they are taking the statement to see whether there is any chance that he or she might be able to say you were entirely, or in part, to blame for the accident.

In Florida, which follows a comparative negligence theory, finding the innocent driver with any portion of the blame will pay substantial dividends for insurance firms. For example, the company handles 1,000 car crash claims per year and the average award per claim is $7,500—that is $7,500,000 in overall compensation. If they can find the victim was 20 percent at fault on those wrecks, that's a $1,500,000 savings a year. That is more than enough money to buy some tv ads to convince you all over again how much they are on your side.

Like A Good Neighbor

The insurance adjusters can be polite to victims of an accident, or they can be rude. They can regularly call, or they may not call at all (and can't be reached). They may give a quick settlement (for a very small amount), or they may play hardball. The behavior of the adjusters is determined by 1) their internal policy, 2) their load of cases and 3) their personality.

The point is - while they act nice and supportive, it's not because they really care about you; it's because they really want to get you to accept the lowest settlement offer possible.

Still, victims of car accidents are lulled into a false sense of security by "caring" adjusters. They then proceed to seek medical care and submit the bills to the adjuster. The adjuster then continues to allow the bills to sit on their desk and gather dust. It is not uncommon to hear people say they thought the at-fault party's adjustor was paying all their medical bills. This charade continues on for several months, before the injured person receives a notice of collection in the mail. The adjuster then has the person right where they want them to — desperate and reliant on their offer to get out of debt from their low-ball settlement. The adjustor's usual response? "I said I should pay the bills not that I would pay the bills."

It would be unfair to paint all adjustors as robots

lacking authentic emotion. Often, their sympathetic expressions are genuine. Nevertheless, even true remorse won't overcome their duty to get their employer out of the lawsuit as cheaply as possible.

They excel at gaining your confidence and trust. If a claim for the damage to your car is resolved quickly and easily, then you assume that their claim for injuries will be resolved equally as efficiently. The thinking is: "If it was so easy to fix my vehicle, they would definitely do the same when it comes to settling my injury claim." It is an idea that insurance firms are promoting and it's just part of their plan.

Unfortunately, this line of reasoning does not play out. Simple resolution of a claim for harm to property doesn't mean easy resolution of the claim for injury to the body, even if the fault is apparent. If the property damage claim is resolved quickly and to the satisfaction of the claimant, the claimant is then pleased and convinced that the company is interested in a fair and favorable solution, which means that the company will pay less on the injury claim.

On the other side, some adjusters often act mean and

cruel and seek to make you feel bad about making a claim. This method works, too. Many people just give up and knuckle under the tough tactics. They just find that the hassle is not worth it all. Some do feel very bad about making a claim on their policy. We subconsciously do not want to be identified as one of the so-called "fakers" who are so prevalent in the stories told by the insurance company. People who are injured in wrecks sometimes feel that everyone will think they are exaggerating their injuries even though they're really hurt. Rather than speaking up for their rights, these people feel guilty and would rather settle for something they know is unjust, just to avoid being thought of in an unfavorable light. Insurance companies love this way of thinking which is why when they catch someone lying about their injuries, they highlight it and make it a big deal.

People trying to lie their way through a personal injury claim is not a common occurrence, yet the insurance companies feed this myth by publicizing a faker when one is caught. Making the general public believe that fraud is rampant 1) poisons juries against someone involved in a wreck; 2) makes people legitimately hurt feel guilty about making a claim; and 3) helps insurance carriers get lawmakers on their side so new, insurance friendly laws can be enacted.

All the jingles, promises, and one-liners will not guarantee you are compensated fairly as a victim. Instead, they are intended in drawing you into a falsely held belief that the insurance company has your best interest at heart. It is a siren's song and falling for it can be a Deadly Sin impacting the just resolution of your claim!

Deadly Sin 5 - Signing Documents You Do Not Understand

Immediately following an injury-related incident, the at-fault insurance company may send you a stack of documents related to the accident. The paperwork will be marked as a "release" and/or "authorization," and will ask for your signature. Before signing the paperwork that the insurance provider sends to you, let's take a deeper look at each of these documents, examine their intent, and how they may impact your accident claim's value drastically. Signing one of these without understanding the ramifications might be a Deadly Sin!

The types of authorizations and approvals may receive and need to understand include:

1. Medical Records Release-Allows the insurance provider to dig into your medical records.

2. Release of All Liability and Claims — Lets the insurance provider "off the hook."

3. Release of Property Damage Form or a Check — Depending on the amount of harm done to the car, your vehicle will either be totaled (and a check for its value sent) or repaired.

To make sure you understand each form, we will review what they mean and address the implications of signing one too soon and/or without an accident attorney first reviewing the claim.

Medical Record Release

Your actual injuries sustained, and the specific medical care needed, should be the primary consideration used to assess the validity of your personal injury case. It is the duty of the insurance provider of the responsible party to compensate you for your medical costs, lost income, and pain and suffering when someone else is at fault for an accident that has caused you to be injured. However, when working with an insurance company, there are no promises that will be the case, because when you sign their medical records release, it allows them access to all of your medical records, past included. This may mean that you're placing your claim at risk, maybe leaving you with nothing.

How would this be a Deadly Sin that could damage your medical claim?

Previous Medical Records

The signing of a medical authorization to gather all your medical records will also allow the insurance company to view previous medical history long before the date of the accident.

Why do they want details like this? Because the insurance company will seek to link your current injuries to what they uncover from your previous health history.

Let's assume that the accident left you with a broken rotator cuff. While mining your medical records, the adjuster finds that you once visited a doctor years before the accident and stated that you had stiffness in the shoulder. They will then use this bit of uncovered knowledge to seek to minimize or refute your claim to injury.

Doctor's Notes

The insurance provider will scour the medical documents from your recent medical visits related to the car accident and check for claims you have made to the doctor that are inconsistent or contradictory with your accident form or post-accident statement. For example, you may have developed headaches as a result of the accident that did not begin until a few days after the incident, but the insurance provider argues that they are not related because you did not mention them on the day of the accident while at the ER.

In the days following the injury, it's very normal to deal with new aches and pains. An accomplished personal injury attorney will be able to tell the story of how the accident changed your quality of life and how the other party's negligence is the cause of your suffering.

Health System Usage

Why do they want to know how often you go to different medical providers?

When you have health conditions unrelated to your accident injury that cause you to see a doctor regularly, or are generally in poor health, the insurance company will paint you as an "eggshell client." What this means is that they would conclude that even though the injuries were caused by the incident, you were medically fragile, and your claim is not as valid. You would not be entitled to damages for what they can prove to be pre-existing, only for what you could prove as having been made worse by the accident.

The best advice is to ask an experienced personal injury to investigate the case before you sign any medical records release authorization.

Release Of All Liability And Claims

It is understandable that victims of someone else's negligence just want to put the whole thing behind them as soon as possible. They want to get better, get their car back, and more importantly, get their life back. Last thing they want to do is drag this on for years. They just want to settle the claim and get what they deserve. However, the difference between a fair payout and a minimum-value payout can depend on whether or not you hired an experienced personal injury lawyer who can advise you on the appropriateness of the insurance company offer.

It is not uncommon to see victims of auto accidents sign a liability release without understanding what the full intent or implications of placing their signature on the paper. Once signed, that release is set in stone. As soon as it is accepted by the insurance accompany, the claim is closed for good and nothing, minus some very rare legal happens, will open it back up.

Generally speaking, any document that is asking you to eliminate all responsibility from the insurance company should be the final paper you sign as a condition of an overall settlement. This is a document that can be prepared by a qualified attorney to protect your best interest. Without an attorney, you will be forced to sign an agreement developed by the insurance company.

Common Things Found In A Release Of All Liability And Claims

The number of people on a release can vary but you should expect to see the following parties named on a release of liability:

- The injured party, i.e. you
- The defendant(s), i.e. the person who hit you and/or the car owner
- The defendant(s) insurance company, e.g. State Farm, Geico, Progressive, etc.

It is recommended that you always contact a personal injury attorney BEFORE signing a liability release to avoid making this Deadly Sin!

Release Of Property Damage Form Or A Check

If you're like most of my clients, replacement / repair of your car, truck or motorcycle is one of your immediate worries. Not only is going without transportation an inconvenience for daily life, but now that you've been involved in an accident, it's imperative that you make all your doctor's appointments, so not having a car will that even more of a challenge.

When it comes to the property damage, the resolution primarily happens either by a payment of fair market value to you or the lien holder, or by direct payment to the repair shop. How this will play out is decided by the insurance company's determination as to the condition of your car.

Your Car Is Totaled

When the damage done to the car is determined to surpass its market value, the insurance provider must make an offer based on the vehicle's current market value in its pre-accident state. You will receive a check and release from the insurance provider for that determined amount. Once the check is cashed (or the release is signed), the claim for damage to property will be closed. Keep in mind that if you have a loan on the vehicle, it is common for the insurance check to be less than the loan's pay-off amount. This is why gap insurance is important on your car loan. It will cover the amount you are up-side down on your loan.

Your Car Is Able To Be Repaired

When the insurance adjuster determines that the damage to your car can be repaired, you are entitled to have the repairs to your car done at the body shop of your choosing. Normally, if the car is not destroyed there will be no release or check sent to you. Instead, the insurance company will pay the repair costs directly to the body shop for all the necessary repairs specified in their estimate and you'll be asked to sign off on the work. If you feel the car is not functioning correctly, you can seek a second opinion or bring the car back to the shop that did the repairs. Make sure the repair is to your satisfaction!

It is important to note that not all personal injury attorneys will also represent you for your property damage claim. Many will provide guidance as a curtesy if they represent you for a personal injury claim. If your car is totaled, is the fair market value accurately calculated? Do they have the correct year and features of the car? If your car is repaired, can you verify everything on the bill was actually done and does the car drive in pre-accident or better condition? Make sure you are happy with how the property damage is settled and ask your attorney for help if needed!

Deadly Sin 6 - Posting Details On Social Media

It's natural to want to reach out to friends and family after a car accident for assistance, emotional support, or just to wind through your day's events. When you post on Facebook or other social media sites about the accident, you are making public comments that can be used to refute your story. You are opening up ammunition for the insurance company to use to try and reject or limit your claim. Do not be fooled … nothing is ever private regardless of how you set up your profile security or privacy levels.

Posting on Facebook following an automobile accident can cause serious damage to your case. It is not just Facebook, other social media sites like Twitter, Instagram, or Snapchat can be mined to be used against you by the insurance company. The goal is to do everything you can to protect your case and get the compensation you deserve for your injuries after a car accident. Innocent posts on social media can be taken out of context or manipulated to try and paint a false story of your injuries. So how do you best handle social media after an accident? The strategy is simple: the best stance is to have nothing to say and nothing to write so as to stay away from this Deadly Sin!

How Are You Being Tracked?

When you initiate a lawsuit, odds are high that you will be checked on social media by someone from the insurance company or the opposing party. Even if your profile is private, they have ways of finding out what you post. There is a lot of money in denying or limiting your claim by twisting your social media content against you. The conclusions they try to make do not have to be true, they just have to create enough doubt. How could your social media posts hurt your case? Here are a few ways:

They Use Details About Your Activities To Say That You Are Not Hurt

A social media post showing you in your garden, on vacation, or even just hanging out at a BBQ in the backyard may be seen as proof that your injuries are not as bad as you say – even though you were just standing in the garden for a few minutes or gritting your teeth to get through the party. The full context is not presented because they have enough to call your pain and injury into question. Maybe that cruise you were leaving on the next day was nonrefundable so you decided to try and make it happen instead of losing the money. That picture of you on the beach in front of the parasailing equipment can harm your case even though you suffered the whole trip.

Statements You Post May Be Read As Your Liability Admission

Fault in a car accident can be a complicated issue to

untangle. Your casual observations about what happened in the accident, like "I've never saw him coming!" or "My old piece of junk car caused the crash!" are singled out as proof that you share some or all of the blame. Insurance adjusters and opposing lawyers will make your statement seem to mean that you accept liability even though you are not legally liable for the accident.

Posting "Too Much" Can Be Used To Say That You Have Not Experienced Emotional Distress

Car crashes can be frightening, and severe injuries can be devastating. The physical suffering and mental trauma may last a lifetime. When you continue to post cheerfully on your social media profiles like nothing happened, an insurance provider may try to argue that the accident didn't affect you as badly as you are claiming, so you don't deserve compensation for the damage you say you experienced.

Speaking About Your Case Can Void Confidentiality

When you post details about your accident and case

online, it is now part of the public domain and knowledge. You lose some of the legal protections you have regarding your confidential information. The privilege you have that protects your conversations with your attorney may suffer because the details are already out in the public and are now fair game. Since car accidents frequently include confidential medical and financial details, keeping updates about your case to yourself is best.

Insurance Company Bad-Mouthing May Be Read As A Sign Of Bad Faith

When we are engaged in a prolonged insurance claim battle, we all want to vent our frustrations. But if you put your grievances online in writing, the insurance company can try to claim that you are not bargaining in good faith – and the insurer will therefore not have to negotiate with you at all. Do not assume that since you have your settings set to "personal" or "friends only" on Facebook, Twitter, or another site, everything you post on such platforms is private. It all has the potential to become public – and to be used by insurance adjusters to reject your claim.

How Do I Deal With Social Media After An Accident?

What are the safest ways to navigate social media following a traffic accident so as to avoid the many possible "traps"? If you must post on social media, and cannot avoid them all together, consider these tips:

- Make your social media accounts private and limit your visibility to only your current friends so only they can see what you're sharing. If the platform allows you to discourage friends from commenting or sharing on your social media stream, trigger these safeguards too. This is not foolproof but may provide minimal protection.

- Stop accepting new friends or followers unless you know them and have full confidence that are who they say they are. Never add an insurance adjuster or an employee of an insurance firm.

- Ideally you would avoid posting entirely before your case is settled. If you must post, never mention your accident or discuss your injuries or emotional state.

Privately notify trusted friends and family and warn them not to post about the accident or your condition as well.

Private Profiles Are Not Private

You may be under the impression that making your Facebook or Twitter accounts "private" might prevent someone from pulling details from those accounts and using them against you in court. This is incorrect. Limiting public access to your social media accounts doesn't stop insurance companies from accessing your Facebook, Twitter, Instagram, Flickr or other social media accounts. Defense attorneys can often view private messages and, in some cases, posts that you have deleted.

This does not mean that if you intend to keep your social media accounts active after the accident, you must avoid any of the public aspects but you should limit access as much as you can. Privacy settings, for example, can help prevent other users from tagging you in pictures or sharing information on their social media accounts. These are the minimum precautions you should take if you are determined to remain online.

When I strongly suggest that you can stop all social media posting, I am not only referring to comments directly about your accident. Suppose, for example, that you're seeking compensation for whiplash injuries suffered in a car accident in Tampa. Now let's say you've posted on Facebook that you are heading to Orlando for some shopping. The prosecution might argue that if you were living with whiplash injuries you would not have been able to drive. Or if you posted a photo of yourself on a nature hike, the insurance company's attorney could try to use the picture to claim that your injuries were not serious enough to keep you from walking.

Can Your Social Media By Subpoenaed?

Could your social media page be subpoenaed by the defense to be used to establish their case in court? Absolutely. The investigation could allow the insurance companies to subpoena any social media platform that may include your data.

The primary federal legislation pertaining to

information disclosure of social media networks is the Stored Communications Act, which is part of the wider Electronic Communications Privacy Act. The legislation does not, however, make social media messages confidential when it comes to discovery in a case involving an accident.

Being Tagged In Pictures

You need to have full control over how and when you appear online. If other members of the social media site have the opportunity to tag you in photographs without your permission, you might not be aware of the pictures you are in after the accident. It is not uncommon for the defense to follow your social media footprint and look for your activity on the pages of your family and friends. The bottom line is that if you keep your social media accounts active, make sure you have privacy settings in place to prevent anyone from tagging your photos on any social networking platforms, or mentioning you.

It is best not to be tagged at grandma's birthday party, laying out at the beach, or even picking up a child!

Removing Social Media Posts

As a final, but important point, do not remove old posts off your social media page that you think may be harmful to your case! This would be destruction of evidence and could get you in trouble with the courts. Nothing is ever really gone and there is always some sort of audit trail that could be subpoenaed to show that you were removing evidence. Instead, seek out a personal injury attorney who could help you best plan on how to account for the possible complications the post may pose for your case. A good attorney will help figure out a solid strategy!

To avoid this Deadly Sin: don't take anything off but also don't provide future evidence!

Deadly Sin 7 - Not Hiring An Attorney!

One of the biggest decisions you will need to make after you are the victim of another's negligence in an accident is whether you should hire an attorney. When you talk to an insurance company, you may find it confusing, complicated, or if you are like most people, you may just find it a hassle and you want to move onto another task. These are all reasons why it may be helpful to have an attorney working for you that will deal directly with the insurance company on your behalf.

Make no mistake – insurance companies will treat

those without an attorney differently than those with legal representation. They can employ an entirely different style of negotiations with those that do not have an experienced personal injury attorney on their side. There are some tried and true tactics used by the insurance companies against those that "go it alone."

Insurance firms are corporations for profit. They aim to make money, not make friends, and insurance companies don't make money when they pay you money. They will do whatever they can to prevent giving you money. Whereas a representative of an insurance company can claim to be your friend, remember the basic truth — insurance companies want to pay you as little as possible so they can hold onto more money for themselves. In fact, representatives of certain insurance companies may get paid more if they pay you less.

In fact, not hiring a personal injury attorney to be on your side and go into battle with you may be the greatest Deadly Sin you could commit!

Tricks So No Treat

Many people aren't prepared for the tricks that insurance companies use in avoiding paying out a deserved sum for accident injuries. The U.S. insurance sector is rich — the sector has trillions of dollars in assets and revenues in excess of $30 billion per year. Its chief executives benefit more than those in other sectors. Insurance companies didn't get this wealthy by paying justifiable compensation to injured people — they got this wealthy by retaining as much of the premium dollars that they can.

How do they get away with it? By employing some of these common tricks:

Deny Your Car Accident Report Outright

Is an accident always an accident? Not if an insurance company can find a way to get out of calling your incident an accident. They can do more than shift the blame, they can make the argument that your accident was no such thing and instead was a deliberate act. The adjustor may look for something in your life or in the facts of the crash to say that the result was intentional so that your claim is denied. Even worse, they can try to say by making a claim, you were fraudulent. While shifting blame or delaying your claim are expected, total denial for an obvious accident often catches victims off-guard.

Staff Incentives

Many times, insurance claims adjustors are rewarded for hitting certain job-based goals. These numbers are not usually geared towards providing their insurers help in their time of need but instead are grounded in attaining low payments for claims. It may be as simple as offering a pizza party to the team that pays out the least amount per claim for the month or other incentives related to pay out vs policy limits. This industry practice to reward employees for undercompensating the injured is one of their tricks and why you need a personal injury attorney on your side.

The Quick Settlement

It is quite common, prior to getting an attorney on board to represent you, that the adjustor will offer you money to take care of your medical expenses. This may be done by sending you a check and is often done by pressuring you to say "yes" on a recorded line. As already discussed, don't sign anything without the advice of an attorney! Trust me when I say that the amount they are offering you will be nowhere near the amount needed to cover the medical care you will need to be made whole. While the $1000 (or even $5000) they are offering today sounds reasonable, that may not be enough to cover one diagnostic test let along an entire course of treatment. This offer is usual made without the adjustor even having a complete picture of your injuries! So how could they possibly know how much money you need to make yourself whole one week after the accident?

They Know You Don't Want To Go To Court

From day one, it is important to have the mindset that every interaction is building towards a court date, even though the intention is to resolve the case without going to court. The possibility of the case moving forward towards a trial is one of the victim's best weapons. If the insurance company thinks you (and your lawyer) are prepared and ready to go to court, then they know they have to pay you the full sum. If the insurance company feels you are unable or unwilling to take it all the way to court if needed, they will look to short-change you on a settlement. Why would they use this to their advantage? If an injured person is reluctant or unable to take the case to court, then the insurance knows they have the upper hand when negotiating and will keep their offer low.

The insurance company is not going to make this strategy known to you. They want you to believe they'll do what's fair, and pay the full amount of a lawsuit, even though they know you are not willing to take the case to court. This goes directly towards their goals. Make as much money for themselves that they can make even if it means lowballing their own client.

That's Why You Have Health Insurance

Auto insurance companies have also been known to claim that if the medical costs have been covered by a private insurance provider or a worker's compensation policy, then the auto insurer does not have to reimburse you for them. This is the exact opposite of how it works in Florida. Our state is a no-fault state and by law, each driver has personal injury protection on their insurance policy. This $10,000 (and possibly more if you have elected for the additional coverage), is your primary insurance for auto accident-related injuries. Only after this money is gone does other insurance become an option.

Here's something else the auto insurance companies won't tell you — after your case is done, the health insurance provider or worker's compensation insurer will place a lien on your settlement and say that you've got to pay them back for the medical services they covered. This process is known as subrogation and could greatly impact your settlement.

Casually Ignore Some Medical Bills

Medical care providers such as clinics, physicians or surgical centers send out their bills in odd ways. For example, if you go to the emergency room, you're likely to get several bills from just one visit. You might get one bill from the ambulance service, a second bill from the hospital and give a third bill from the ER doctors. Surgeries operate the same way: the doctor who performed the operation will send one bill, a second bill will be sent from the hospital or facility where the procedure was done, and the anesthesiologist will possibly send a third. Your insurance company should take care of all the bills related to your accident.

The insurance companies know that they need to pay all the bills and they know that medical bills are often separated this way, but they still will neglect to make sure they have a complete picture of what is out there. They will acknowledge a few bills and then tell you they have taken care of your bills. You may not find out until after the case has been resolved that the insurance company hasn't paid all the expenses it was supposed to pay. At that time, it is too late. You should have had an attorney on your side.

Causation Defense

The insurance adjustor may pretend to be your friend

and may seem to be genuinely concerned for your health, and there are many who truly are. They may make you promises that they will make everything work for your benefit. But later in the process, they may pull the so-called "causation" defense. This means that they're trying to say that anything other than the actual accident caused your injury, and that they shouldn't have to pay you the full sum (if any).

Even when liability may seem so obvious – the other driver verbally admits fault or the police report plainly says who was at fault – getting the compensation for your injuries may not be as easy. They are going to search through your medical history, hoping to find a medical report from somewhere in your background that they can claim proves you've always had this injury. Or they will argue that what caused the injury is something that happened after and unrelated to the accident so they shouldn't have to pay for it. Often, they clearly imply that it is your age (and the aging process) that is the cause of your ailing back. In certain cases, the insurance company will employ a radiologist — that is, someone who reads MRIs — to analyze the MRI and say the injury looks old, so this incident must not have caused it. Insurance firms pay hundreds of thousands of dollars (or even millions of dollars over the years) to these radiologists, and some dishonest radiologists can say pretty much whatever the insurance companies want. The insurance company has doctors on their side that will seek to discredit your neutral, third-party medical provider.

Use Your Politeness Against You

After an accident, being respectful and considerate for the other person is reasonable, even though that person was at fault. Unfortunately, even if you tell the other party not to worry about the crash or kindly say that it was not the fault of the other party, their insurance provider might seek to use your kindness against you. The insurance company could argue that your comment meant you weren't really hurt or admitted to some fault — even if you didn't mean that.

Even if the incident is obviously not your fault, Florida is a state of pure comparative negligence, meaning your payout would be decreased by the amount that you are to blame. The insurance company of the other party will do all they can to prove you are partially at fault, because this reduces their payout. Or put it another way, the insurance provider collects more money for itself by accusing you.

Apply Pressure

Shortly after a crash, both your insurance company and the insurance company of the other party may contact you. The insurance company will pressure you to accept a low payout which is unlikely to cover your actual expenses, and those expenses will continue to roll in. They will make note of what you say in hopes that they could later find something to use against you.

You will be told by the insurance adjuster that you should approve a settlement agreement by a specified date. Do not. Insurance companies will tell people who have no attorney this because they are trying to get the injured person to settle their claim before they have a chance to find a decent lawyer. When an injured individual hires a lawyer, the insurance firm knows there's going to be more to pay.

Demand A Recorded Statement

The insurance company may request that you submit a written or documented statement within a stated time span. The insurance adjuster can inform you before you make a statement that they cannot start their claims process. While you may have to talk to your own insurance due to the rules of your policy, you can do so with an attorney by your side. When it comes to the at-fault party's insurance company, be even more cautious. The insurance company will ask leading questions to get you talking in hopes of getting you to say something they can use against your case later.

Consider consulting a good personal injury lawyer in Florida before you talk to the insurance company. You have the right to speak with an attorney before giving the insurance company any statement, whether recorded or not. Don't make a comment about the accident when you're still upset, angry, or emotional.

When you make a comment shortly after an incident, some of your injuries may still not be evident and other signs can be obscured by the initial shock and discomfort. Later, when doctors discover more injuries, or when new pain starts to occur, and you tell the insurance provider about the medical problems, the insurance company may argue that you lied and that these recent problems were not related to the accident.

You don't need to make a statement before the insurance company's deadline. You do have the right to speak to an attorney before you speak to the insurance company. Make sure you do!

Acting Like Your Friend

Insurance representatives are not your friend. As previously discussed, adjusters may seek to compromise early and then act as if by agreeing to pay your medical bills that have come in so far, and by tossing in a few thousand dollars more, they are giving you a great deal. Is that really a deal? How about future medical bills? Your future earning potential that you may lose?

Lost jobs, or the vacation and sick days you've had to take?

You are only allowed to settle once. After a settlement, you can't 'reopen' the case or seek extra money if the condition gets worse or begins acting up again. Know your rights. If an insurance provider says, "early settlement," it most always means "lowball settlement."

Save You from The Attorney

To keep you from talking to a good lawyer, insurance companies sometimes say that they are going to "accept blame" or "accept responsibility" and pay the bills. What the insurance company doesn't tell you is they will have to "admit fault" anyway, particularly if you were rear-ended or if the police officer gave the other driver a ticket. You may also not be told by the insurance company that they will try to avoid paying for your future medical bills, for your pain and suffering, or even for the full amount of your past medical bills. They will "admit blame," but they will nickel-and-dime you to pay you the least amount possible.

Insurance companies sometimes say that you should

not hire a lawyer because "lawyers charge too much" or "a smart person like you doesn't need their help." This should clue you into their true intentions and where their loyalty resides. They try to discourage you from hiring an attorney so that they will not have to pay more if you actually find a competent personal injury lawyer.

Delay Your Settlement

An insurance company wins by delaying your settlement. Every day your settlement is pushed off, they benefit by:

1. Holding onto the money longer so instead of you earning interest they do.

2. As time goes by, and medical bills grow and you become desperate for cash, the chances of you expecting a low offer increase.

3. Eventually, if they wait long and you do not act, the statute of limitations shall expire, at which point you shall forfeit all your rights to sue for your injuries. In Florida, the

statute of limitations for a personal injury claim is four years.

Your friend the insurance company will send out small sums of money to keep you happy in the hopes that you do not call an attorney who will know the value of your claim. You could be given a check by the insurer to repair the vehicle, but not a check to cover the full current and potential medical costs.

The insurance adjustor will offer to get and review more of your medical records so they can have the complete picture on how to help you. They will promise to do their hardest to close the case and pay you what you deserve. After you supply them with the records, they will tell you that they need some more details before they can finalize your full payment. When you call, they just might not reply or pick up their phone, leaving you wondering about what's going on with your situation.

Question Your Medical Treatment

Your doctors will recommend a specific course of treatment and the insurance company may question it. They may question the therapies and the testing your doctor has ordered. If you are getting a lot of medical care, the insurance company may claim that you don't need it, and instead insist that it is only to milk the system. If you are not treating enough, they may tell you that your injuries are minor and so is your claim.

If you're injured, see your doctor right away. You have only one body. Many times people want to put off seeing the doctor in hopes of 'toughing it out', trusting that their injuries will heal on their own. When you wait to see a doctor or change your mind after stubbornly deciding not to initially, the insurance company assumes your injury must not have been that serious. The insurance company also now has the door opened for them to claim that any injuries diagnosed by the doctor were not from the crash but may have happened after the accident. Even a delay of a few days can present the insurance company with an opportunity to question your injuries. Remember in Florida, you have fourteen days to seek medical care for your injuries to be able to make a claim against the insurance company.

Insurance companies often blame injuries sustained in accidents on what they term "pre-existing conditions." Essentially, what this means is that the insurance company is taking the stance that you had the injuries you are reporting as resulting from the accident actually happened the accident. This will be used to argue why they should not have to pay beyond a minimal amount. This line of reasoning has certain weight if you re-injured a particular part of the body in the incident. For example, if after a car accident you have pain in your right shoulder, and this is the same shoulder you previously had surgery on several years prior, they will seek to link your current pain to the pre-accident surgery.

Once again it is important to repeat this – do not sign something that gives broad, general permission to the insurance company to be able to search into all your past medical history so they can try to find something irrelevant to reduce the legitimacy of your claim. Your claim should be based on your current injuries and pain. The day before the accident you felt a certain way and then the day of (or in the many days after), you feel an entirely different way.

Do not sign anything giving the insurance company carte blanche power until speaking to an attorney.

They May Spy On You

The insurance company does not limit their determination only to the facts of your accident and your medical records to make the right decision. If your case warrants it because of the amount of possible compensation, an investigator can be assigned to try to get hidden video footage of you as you leave your home, trying to find something they can use against you. This surveillance, or spying, may be to try and catch you taking out the trash or playing a round of golf. Something as innocent as lifting your toddler may be used against you. Insurance companies can also spy on your social media in the hope that they may find a picture, video, or comment to use against you.

What can a good attorney do? If they have determined

that the insurance company did spy on you, your attorney can go on the offensive. One of the first things you can do is demand that the spy appear for a deposition to be questioned under oath (they are not fond of this). If the claim goes to trial, a good attorney then can cross-examine the spy in front of the jury. The insurance company has a team of people and will play many tricks – make sure you have someone on your side that knows how to protect you from insurance company games.

Innocently Misquote Your Coverage

Don't take an insurance company employee's word for it when they tell you about your policy. Make sure you have the information in front of you to follow along and ask questions. Even better, have an experienced personal injury attorney on your side to advise you on your options.

Insurance plans can be confusing and insurance companies sometimes count on you not understanding everything you are entitled to in your policy. You pay your premiums to help you during these times. Make sure you are getting the benefit of your preparation. A good lawyer with personal injury experience can help you untangle the complex legal and policy issues.

Not hiring a personal injury attorney is the most cardinal Deadly Sin! It is the one that could have the greatest impact on you being justly compensated for your injuries. Do your research today and add an experienced personal injury firm to your contact list so they can be one of your first phone calls after an accident!

Conclusion

An automobile accident raises a host of concerns. Who is to blame? Who pays for the damage to my car? Who is going to pay for my medical bills? How much compensation will I be getting? Should I expect the insurance company to help me with missed wages?

In this book, we have examined 7 Deadly Sins that you may commit which will make the answer to those questions more complicated. The key to being justly compensated for your injuries often lies in hiring a good personal injury lawyer. An experienced injury attorney can be particularly helpful in negotiating the pitfalls around these types of cases which are sometimes complicated and confusing. Let's spend some time looking at how you should go about hiring the right attorney for your case.

How To Find The Right Attorney

Do not expect to find the right attorney by flipping open the phone book. It is not that simply. While that was prevalent years ago, and I am not certain it worked, today you may need to take a different approach.

Personal Referrals

Talk to people in your circle – family and friends – to gather information on their experience and results. Make sure you focus on recommendations of those that had a personal experience in a similar type of case. Do not rely solely on a personal referral but use this as a basis to move to the next step of meeting and discussing your case. Ultimately, you need to feel comfortable working with the person you choose. Knowing someone you trust has had a positive experience with a particular attorney may make it more likely you will have that positive relationship as well.

Online Directory

There are many sites where you can search for a lawyer who works in a particular area of law and read reviews from former clients. You can often learn about their education and time spent as an attorney. From these sites, you may be able to contact the attorney directly or go to their website for more information. Be wary of sites that seem to slick as often attorneys can pay for placement which has nothing to do with the quality of the representation. A good place to start may be that of your local chamber of commerce or the Florida Bar.

Business Referrals

Similar to personal referrals, you can seek out other business professionals you trust – your accountant, banker, doctor – and ask them about their experience and who they would recommend. These folks frequently come into contact with many attorneys and have developed strong opinions on things such as professionalism and work ethic. They may even see the less "public" face as they interact with local attorneys on a different level. While sometimes there may be other motives involved, if you have a good business relationship with someone, the hope is that they would value that and will want to refer you to someone who would have the same concern.

How To Decide Who To Hire

You will be deciding to enter into a relationship so make sure you have a level of comfort with the person you are choosing. Set up a meeting so you can discuss your case details. Focus on the chemistry between yourself and the attorney. Discuss communication and how you will be kept informed of what is going on with your case. Trust your instincts and make an informed decision.

Expertise In Law And Rules Of Procedure

Hiring a personal injury lawyer to represent you following a car accident means you will have a specialist working for you — one that is highly knowledgeable about the relevant laws and legal rules that can impact your case.

An attorney may notify you about any time considerations (called statutes of limitations) that can prohibit you from filing a complaint against the at fault driver. For example, in Florida you have to file your lawsuit within four years of your car accident or you will be prohibited from filing your lawsuit forever. An attorney will also be able to inform you, for example, of any special exceptions to the statute of limitations — i.e., for minors.

Your attorney will work on your behalf and should be able to help overcome any potential defenses that the other side might claim. Moreover, once your case gets under way, your lawyer will play an invaluable role in preparing your case for trial — and often even go to trial if your case is not resolved.

Despite the rare need for a lawsuit, the threat of legal action offers strong leverage when negotiating a fair settlement. You need an attorney that will be able to stand up against a powerful opponent and one who they will respect.

Finally, and perhaps more importantly, having an attorney who is knowledgeable about the law levels the playing field, particularly when you are wrestling with a large insurance company 's experience and vast resources. When you have a capable attorney on your side, you are ready to go toe-to-toe with the insurance company!

Doing The Job

There is a lot of effort that goes into negotiating an insurance settlement and possibly pursuing a personal injury lawsuit. After you've been in a car accident, the last thing you want to do is take on this time-consuming job and the stress it will involve. An attorney will be on your side protecting your interest as your interests are aligned.

Although this could be your first time dealing with the ins and outs of a lawsuit of this nature, an experienced personal injury attorney will have worked all kinds of various injury cases and with different insurance companies. They will have the experience in gathering the necessary documentation to support your case, including obtaining police reports, witness statements, medical records and bills, and facts about jobs and missed wages.

Your attorney will also be able to organize the facts

and put together a compelling demand packet which makes the argument for your just compensation. If you are unable to settle your accident case, your attorney will be able to take care of filing the necessary paperwork to start a court case and represent you when dealing with the defense attorneys. Having someone who is knowledgeable in handling the complexities of your case is particularly important especially if you've been seriously injured and are focused on recovery.

Someone To Defend You

Perhaps the most important way an attorney can help you is by being your advocate. This means that your attorney can work on your behalf and for your benefit during the entire process. He or she will be your voice before the insurance company, judge, jury, and other attorneys, making sure your side of the story is heard and respected.

It is important to have a knowledgeable and persuasive lawyer working with you to secure a just and equitable settlement in your case of a car accident. That person will become your advocate, protector, and guide to navigate what is often a treacherous process. It is your attorney who can assist you from falling into any of the Deadly Sins and help you overcome being a victim.

How To Afford An Attorney

The first question people normally want answered is, "how will I pay for a fancy attorney?" Thankfully the means are often simple. Many car accidents lawyers bill for their services in a relatively unusual manner as compared to the hourly rate that you may be used to from another type of attorney. The typical car accident lawyer charges a "contingency fee" to take on an injury lawsuit. A contingency charge means that no attorney's fees will be owed by you until your case settles. Upon the successful securement of a settlement or jury decision, the law firm will have earned a portion of the money attained.

The percentage of a contingency fee arrangement that a personal injury lawyer may earn varies, but usually ranges from 25 to 40 percent with 33 percent (or one-third) as fairly standard.

If you have an arrangement for a contingency fee of 33% and you recover $120,000 in your accident case, your attorney will receive about $40,000.

It is always important to discuss the contingency fee with your attorney, and to carefully review your legal services contract. The contingency fee contract must be in writing. If you do not understand the contract fee arrangement, ask your attorney to explain it to you.

Being in an accident is a scary and confusing time. It is my hope that this book in some way helps you understand the Florida personal injury process and the things you must be mindful of and try to avoid. This is not a battle between good and bad; it is a jousting of competing interests.

Let this book help put you on the offensive.

Brian

About The Author

Attorney Brian S. Brijbag has been admitted to practice law in the State of Florida and has over 20 years of experience in personal injury having worked in the medical field in multiple roles. Brian is a longtime resident of the Nature Coast of Florida and now enjoys raising his family in the community. Brian is the author of *7 Deadly Sins of Your Florida Personal Injury Case: A Victim's Guide to Florida Personal Injury Claims* as well as the author of *Southern Chivalry: Environmental Hazard Risk Communication and Perception in a Small Southern Neighborhood.*

Attorney Brijbag received his Juris Doctor from Western Michigan University T.M. Cooley Law School while also having a Master Degree of Public Health, Master Degree of Applied Anthropology, Bachelor of Arts in Applied Anthropology, and Bachelor of Arts in Religious Studies from the University of South Florida.

To learn more about Attorney Brian S. Brijbag, please visit:

www.brijbaglaw.com

Or on Twitter at:

www.twitter.com/brianbrijbag